HISTORY

OF THE TOWN OF

BERKLEY, MASS.,

INCLUDING SKETCHES OF THE LIVES OF THE TWO
FIRST MINISTERS,

Rev. SAMUEL TOBEY,

AND

Rev. THOMAS ANDROS,

WHOSE UNITED MINISTRY CONTINUED NINETY-ONE YEARS.

BY

Rev. ENOCH SANFORD, M. A.,

Member of the Old Colony Historical Society; Corresponding Member of the
New York Genealogical and Biographical Society, and of the State
Historical Society of Wisconsin, etc.

NEW YORK:
KILBOURNE TOMPKINS, PRINTER.

1872.

Notice

In many older books, foxing (or discoloration) occurs and, in some instances, print lightens with wear and age. Reprinted books, such as this, often duplicate these flaws, notwithstanding efforts to reduce or eliminate them. The pages of this reprint have been digitally enhanced and, where possible, the flaws eliminated in order to provide clarity of content and a pleasant reading experience.

Originally published
New York
1872

Reprinted by:

Janaway Publishing, Inc.
732 Kelsey Ct.
Santa Maria, CA 93454
(805) 925-1038
www.JanawayGenealogy.com

2018

ISBN: 978-1-59641-423-5

Made in the United States of America

All those things which are now held to be of the greatest antiquity were at one time new: and what we, to-day, hold up by example, will rank hereafter as a precedent.

—*Tacitus.*

NOTE.

The writer, having a personal acquaintance with the inhabitants of the town of Berkley, and its affairs, continuing for a period of more than three-quarters of a century, at the request of friends, has prepared the following pages.

In their preparation he has sought to chronicle matters of merely local value, in a style and phraseology in accord with the importance of the topics discussed.

The Manse, Raynham, Ms.
October 26th, A. D., 1871

HISTORY.

Anno Regni Regis Georgii Secundi Octavo.
Eighth year of the reign of King George II.

AN ACT for dividing Towns of Taunton and Dighton, erecting a new town there by the name of Berkley.

Whereas the southerly part of Taunton and the northerly part of Dighton, on the east side of the great river, is competently filled with inhabitants who labor under difficulties by reason of the remoteness from the places of public meetings in the said towns, and have thereupon made application to this Court that they may be set off a different and separate parish, and be vested with all the powers and privileges that other towns in this Province are vested with,

Be it therefore enacted by his Excellency the Governor, Council, and Representatives in General Court assembled, and by the authority of the same, that the southerly part of Taunton and northerly part of Dighton, on the east side of the great river as hereafter bounded be, and hereby are, set off, constituted and erected into a separate and distinct township by the name of Berkley. (Then the bounds are given.) And the inhabitants thereof be, and hereby are, vested and endowed with equal powers and privileges and immunities that the inhabitants of any of the towns within this Province are by law vested with.

Only it is to be understood, and the inhabitants of the town of Berkley are hereby requested, within the space of two years from the publication of this act, to procure and settle a learned and orthodox minister, of good conversation, and make provision for his comfortable and honorable support, and also erect and finish a suitable and convenient house for the public Worship of God, in said town.

Another proviso in the Act is, that the town shall from time to time pay towards the repairs of Weir bridge their proportion with Taunton, and all arrears of debts.

April the 18th, 1735. This Bill having been read three several times in the House of Representatives passed to be enacted.

J. QUINCY, *Speaker.*

April 18th, 1735. This bill having been read three several times in Council, passed to be enacted.

T. MASON, *Dep. Sec'y.*

By his Excellency the Governor:—
I consent to the enacting this Bill.

J. BELCHER.

This town was named after Bishop Berkeley who resided at Newport, R. I., in 1729–31 and died 1753, and was famous for the evangelic benevolence of his character and the acuteness of his genius. His mind was ever full of projects for increasing the virtue and happiness of his fellow creatures. One was the establishment of a missionary college in the Bermudas. For that purpose he came to America and consulted with many of the principal men respecting his enterprise. He was Bishop of Cloyne in Ireland, and presents one of the rare instances of a prelate obstinately refusing any further promotion out of pure love to his flock. He was the author of the Minute Philosopher, and other works and poems, among them that well known ode, the last stanza of which begins—

"Westward the course of empire takes its way."

When he heard that this town had taken his name he donated a church organ to it and sent it to Newport. But certain of the inhabitants were opposed to instrumental music in churches, and money could not be raised to pay the freight, and there it remained till some persons claimed it in payment of storage. Many years afterwards there were some who would not tolerate musical instruments in the choir. When the bass viol first began to be played only in the last singing, Mr. Abner Burt, a prominent man, would rise and, slamming the pew door after him, leave the church, and when asked why he did so, said he would not hear that bull roar. There is no record as alleged that the town voted not to receive Bishop Berkeley's gift for the reason that it was an invention of the devil to catch men's souls.

The first town meeting in Berkley was held May 13th, 1735, at Elkanah Babbitt's house. Gershon Crane was chosen Moderator, and Abel Burt, Town Clerk. Joseph Burt, John Paul, Benaiah Babbit, Selectmen. These and other officers, it was voted, should serve without compensation for their labors. Two tithing men were chosen.

At the second town meeting, legally called Oct. 6th, 1735, the town voted to hire a "scholar" to preach in the town a quarter of a year, and fifty pounds were voted to be raised for his support and other purposes, and it was voted to employ no schoolmaster at present.

At an adjourned meeting, Oct. 20th, 1735, voted to send for Mr. Tobey to come and preach one quarter of a year, and John Burt to take the contribution money towards supplying the scholar, i. e. minister.

Voted to build a meeting house forty feet long and thirty-four feet wide and eighteen feet stud, and that the work of getting timber and building be divided among the inhabitants equally, and each man be allowed four shillings a day, and boys proportionally.

At a meeting of the town, Feb., 1735, voted to continue Mr. Tobey in the work of the ministry. Voted to send to the General Court requesting them to appoint a committee to come and locate the meeting house; but thirty-one persons protested against this and it was not done. Aug., 1736, voted to call Mr. Tobey to the work of the ministry, on a salary of one hundred pounds a year, paper money, and two hundred pounds settlement. Voted, 1737, to assess £250 to enable Samuel Mirick to finish the meeting house.

ORGANIZING THE CHURCH.

This was done Nov. 2d, 1737, twenty-one days before the ordination of their pastor, by Rev. Nathaniel Fisher, Rev. Benjamin Ruggles, probably of Rochester, and Rev. Thomas Clapp of Taunton, with their delegates. The church consisted of the following members:

Rev. Samuel Tobey, Elkanah Babbit, Ebenezer Hathaway, Gersham Crane, John French, Ebenezer Philips, John Briggs, Ephraim Allen, Benjamin Leonard, John Hudson, Josiah Babbit, Benjamin Babbit, George Babbit, Daniel Axtel, Abigail Burt, Mary Philips, Mary Jones, Hopestill Harvey, Hannah French, Experience Myrick, Hopestill Woods, Elizabeth Hathaway, Mercy Babbit, Sarah Briggs, Abigail Babbit, Dorcas Jones, Hopestill Philips, Zippora Allen, Elizabeth Paul, Dorcas Babbit, Witstill Axtell, Phebe Reed, Jemima Hathaway, Abigail Burt 2d.

These thirty-four members had belonged to the church in Dighton and in Taunton. They had been residing for some years in this new settlement, and to enjoy the privileges of public worship had been in the habit of crossing the river by ferry boat to Dighton, or going five miles to Taunton. "They would now have no such lengths to go to wander far abroad." On the same day were united with the church fifteen more by profession, making the members forty-nine, twenty-five males and twenty-four females.

THE FIRST MINISTER.

Rev. Samuel Tobey was a native of Sandwich, a graduate of Harvard College, 1733, in the twenty-second year of his age. August 3, 1736, the people gave him a call to settle with them, a young man having scarcely finished his preparatory studies for his profession, commencing the duties of it in a new settlement, among a farming people scattered over a large territory. But the people required a minister to instruct them and their children. Though their houses are rudely built, the roads rough and unfenced, their fields half broken up and yielding them barely a living, they cannot enjoy the Sabbath or their homes without a man of God among them. How welcome he was may be seen by their offering, in their penury, two hundred pounds for his settlement and a hundred for his salary per year. This he accepted upon their adding the contribution which it was usual to take every Sabbath, and stating his salary at twenty-six shillings per ounce of silver. Thus the people determined to give him a liberal support, that he might devote himself to his work for their benefit; settled him for life, that he might never wish to change his place, and that he might have time, free from care, to improve in all useful knowledge.

Nov. 23, 1737. The ministers officiating in the ordination services were the following:— Rev. Mr. Billings, Rev. Mr. Fisher of Dighton, Rev. Mr. Fessenden, probably of Sandwich, and Rev. John Wales of Raynham. Mr. Wales offered prayer, Mr. Fessenden preached an excellent sermon from the words in Col. 2:5. "Joying and beholding your order." After which Mr. Billings gave the charge, Mr. Fisher the right hand of fellowship, and all was performed, says the brief record, to good acceptance. What a simple but noble beginning was this for the establishing of divine ordinances where a few years before beasts of the wilderness and savages held sway.

Rev. Mr. Tobey was married to Bathsheba Crocker, Sep. 6, 1738, and Oct. 31 they moved into his house, and he writes, "Will God speak well of the house of his servant for a long time to come, and as for me and my household, we will serve the Lord." They were blessed with twelve children, some of whom I shall describe further on. The two youngest were twins—Paul and Silas.

The parsonage which he owned stood a little east of the Park, facing the south, two stories in front and one in the rear, the north roof sloping quite low. This was the style of the best houses of that day. President John Adams occupied such an one in Quincy before he was President. Mr. Tobey owned also a farm of twenty-five or thirty acres which was a great help to him and his family. His house was the resort of clerical friends, his doors were open to visitors and strangers and his hospitality always manifest and unstinted.

As a preacher, he was not brilliant but grave and honest in declaring what he believed true and essential. I have seen several who long sat under his preaching. As a "master of assemblies," he was firm and impartial. He was of a full countenance and uncommonly engaging in his person and manners. All revered him as a man of eminent abilities and of great common sense and unaffected appearance. The children not only revered but loved him, especially when he came into the schools and talked to them as a father. He seemed to regard all the people not only as his flock but as his children.

The structure of his sermons was formal, according to the manner of ministers of that time, who made many divisions of their subjects and rarely went to the opposite extreme now practiced. His style was open and so plain the unlearned could understand and remember the truths uttered.

In his devotional exercises in the pulpit he was somewhat formal, using nearly the same expressions in many of his prayers. That he was edifying and attractive to the common people is evident from the fact that he was highly esteemed in his deportment and public services for nearly three generations, and the older he grew the more he was valued. He usually rode on horseback, and by some accident he fell and was so injured that he lived but a short time after, and died Feb. 13, 1781.

Mr. Tobey was the eighth child of Samuel Tobey and Abia, his wife; born May 8th, 1715. Samuel was the son of Thomas, and grandson of Thomas Tobey, senior, the first of that name in Sandwich.

In 1784, Rev. Daniel Tomlinson was invited to become the pastor. The town voted to concur with the church and settle him on £150 salary. In 1785, Rev. Amos Chase was called by the church, and the town concurred, and offered to build him a two story dwelling house, and give him £85 a year. Both declined, probably on account of the small salary.

After a vacancy of six years Rev. Thomas Andros was invited to preach in this town. April 17, 1787, he came and preached four sabbaths. In June following he came again and tarried four sabbaths more, and received a call to settle, but did not, through distrust of his health, venture to give an answer until Feb., 1788, which he then did in the affirmative. He was ordained 19th March following. "Bishops of the ordaining council" were, Rev. Levi Hart of Preston, Conn., Rev. Dr. Joel Benedict of Plainfield, Conn., Rev. Solomon Morgan of Canterbury, Ct., Rev. Ephraim Judson, Taunton, and Rev. John Smith, Dighton. Rev. Joel Benedict preached from I.Cor. 4:9.

THE SECOND MINISTER, REV. THOMAS ANDROS,

was a native of Norwich, Conn., born May 1, 1754. At the age of eighteen he enlisted in the army of the Revolution, was a soldier and musician more than two years, was captured and confined in the prison ship which lay near Brooklyn, with hundreds of others who were treated with great cruelty. By some fortunate incident he escaped to Long Island, travelled on foot the length of it, and then escaped to Connecticut. The perils and sufferings of this imprisonment and escape he has described in a little book entitled "The Old Jersey Captive," which is now out of print, and ought to be republished.

After recovering his health, he devoted himself to study two or three years with Rev. Joel Benedict, in preparation for the ministry. By a happy Providence, he was led to this part of Massachusetts, and was called to the pastorate of the church and society, and was settled on the salary of £80, which was, perhaps, worth $400, the usual salary of village pastors. But afterwards, as paper money greatly depreciated, it was increased, though a great portion of it was paid in produce at market prices. Under his ministration, the population and church increased. The people, by the war of the Revolution, were much impoverished ; there were no manufactures, except what families carried on for themselves, and farming was almost the only resort.

Mr. Andros, purchased a house and a few acres near the meeting house, where he lived about twenty years. His first wife was Miss Abigail Cutler, of Killingly, Ct. Here she died, leaving him with nine children, the youngest being an infant of a few months. While the funeral services were being performed, the cries of the infant were heard, and melted the large assembly to tears. He occupied his pulpit while his wife's remains were at his home laid out for burial, and afterwards preached her funeral sermon, which was printed. In due time he looked around to find a mother for his children. To find another to fill the vacant place caused him much anxiety and prayer. He at length married Sophia, third daughter of Captain John Sanford, and Sarah Deane, his wife. From her father, who died before her birth, she inherited a farm situated two miles south from the meeting house, on the Freetown Road. She was of amiable character, attractive figure, and better educated than most women at that day. She proved well qualified for the important station she was to fill.

From this marriage there were born to them eight children, which made a numerous family; all of them arriving at adult age. Soon after his second marriage, he sold his residence near the meeting house and moved to his wife's farm, the products of which were of great assistance in the support of his family. The one-story house was raised to two stories. His health, usually feeble, was recruited by morning and evening farm exercise. His children were taught to be industrious, and were early qualified for active business abroad. Their success I shall describe in this history.

When Mr. Andros first settled in Berkley, he had pursued classical studies only to a limited extent. In a few years he acquired such knowledge of the learned languages and of the general sciences as to enable him to instruct young men in their preparation for college. His clear and comprehensive views of the doctrines of the Gospel were appreciated by neighboring pastors and churches. His style in composition, if it had not the polish of later years, showed strong intellectual powers, and a vigor and strength of reasoning scarcely surpassed by any. He had not only studied the best models, but by his own genius, as if aided by inspiration, he laid open the great truths of the Gospel to the apprehension of his hearers.

The influence he exerted, during a ministry of nearly half a century, in raising the standard of education has been acknowledged by the people. He spent much time, though without pecuniary reward, in visiting the several schools, examining teachers and addressing the children, who always regarded him with much reverence, and perhaps some fear, for ministers and learned men were not at that day very accessible to the young.

His published discourses were quite numerous; the funeral sermon on the death of his wife and the "Old Jersey Captive" have been mentioned. He published a sermon on the death of Capt. John Crane, in 1795; one delivered at the funeral of Hon. Samuel Tobey, in 1823; one on the death of Caleb Hathaway; one on Prayer, in 1808; one preached before the Association, entitled "The Church Increased by its own Energies." He published, in 1818, a pamphlet in answer to Rev. Noah Worcester's "Bible News," which was republished some time afterwards by Samuel T. Armstrong; another pamphlet against Rev. Jacob Norton, of Weymouth, who wrote against "Human Creeds." He published a small work on "Divine Agency," in 1820, against those who appear to be verging towards fatalism; also four "Discourses on the Prophecies," preached Fast days; and a sermon at the ordination of Rev. Benjamin Whitmore, Tiverton, R. I. Besides these he published a small volume of six sermons, a sermon on Temperance, one on False Philosophy, in 1819, and several controversial pamphlets.

As a speaker or pulpit orator, he was not superior. But as a thinking and reading people consider more what is spoken, than who it is that speaks or in what manner it is spoken, so he attracted his hearers by the weighty things he uttered. His voice was on a high key, and so piercing it would fill the largest auditorium. He usually preached from notes; but when his mind was roused, he could not be confined to them, but spoke in what Dr. Campbell calls the "vehement" manner.

THE CHARACTER OF HIS PREACHING.

The improvements and modifications in many points of orthodoxy during the seventeenth century received his approbation, and seemed to emanate from his own mind, as may be discovered from his writings. He coincided with the late principal divines of New England, but adhered, as he often said, to what he called the Doctrines of the Reformation. He never preached that Christ made atonement by his death for the elect only, and not for all mankind; or that justifying faith consists in one's believing that his sins are forgiven, and that he is one of the saved; or that man, in regeneration, is as passive as a child in being born into the world; or that man is unable to repent, or that no mere man, since the fall, is able perfectly to keep the divine commands. He is remembered never to have believed or preached that the sin of the first man is imputed to all his posterity, and that in him all sinned, and that each brings sin enough into the world to subject him to the loss of heaven. Neither did he preach that Christ's righteousness is made over or transferred to believers, but rather that he teaches us how we may acquire the righteousness which is acceptable by faith and good works. He strenuously enforced that men have the power of choice, are responsible for their moral acts, that no divine agency operates in men to harden or tempt them to sin, but rather to restrain them from it.

Much of the force of his preaching consisted in the logical order of the main points of his discourse. His thoughts were consecutive, and the force of the argument increased as he proceeded from one point to another. This method, with the plainness of his style, made it easy for every attentive hearer to understand him. The last parts of his discourse were always the most striking, as they were in the direct and not the oblique style, and not made to apply to people anywhere, but to those present before him. Hence, he said, in preparing his discourses, he considered the wants of those to whom they were to be addressed.

He preached once on "Keeping the heart," in which he showed what is meant by it, and by what means it may be kept, and when he appeared to have exhausted the subject he said he would add one thing more, that in order to keep the heart we must give it to God, as He requires; then, for five minutes, he pressed this duty so earnestly the audience were profoundly silent and attentive, and on going out one said, and he doubtless spoke the feeling of others, he could have sat there till sundown. Though his appearance in the pulpit was far from imposing at the first view, yet his freedom and earnestness soon appeared as he proceeded. He soon surmounted all apparent diffidence. So full of thought and truth were his discourses, that they seemed to take the hearers, instead of the hearers taking them. They were elaborated with much care, revised, and many words and sentences struck out before he was satisfied with them. His sermons during fifty years were numerous, embracing all the doctrines and duties of religion. His attainments in this long period were continually increasing, and I have heard him say that his early sermons appeared tame and tasteless.

The chief quality of his style was a singular power of thought and appropriate diction, of which he did not seem conscious. No subject seemed new to him or difficult to explain, and he seemed to manage all subjects with equal ease. A learned scholar who often called on him said he appeared to have just been investigating the subject of conversation introduced. He made difficult subjects so plain and easy that an ordinary preacher might think he could do the same, but in attempting would fail. His sermons had no gloss of embellishments, nor any profusion of images, nor melody of periods which might charm an audience. Nor did he seek to add weight to them by learned quotations from popular writers. He had not room for them, so great was the flow of weighty thoughts from his own mind.

The plainness of his style was remarkable, for he used pure English, never sought for ornaments or metaphors for their own sake, and when he used comparisons they were brief and not run out into simple parallelisms. He was never known to employ witticisms in his discourses, and nothing that approached vulgarity; nothing that had not the stamp of popular use, or the authority of sound writers; nothing unfamiliar to the common ear.

During the latter part of his long ministry, the pulpit had less of a metaphysical character than formerly. Sermons of a controversial kind have been fewer, and greater attention given to Bible studies. Volumes of sermons have been supplanted by a greater number of tracts. Mr. Andros always co-operated with the rising benevolent societies of the day, which have tended greatly to remove the prejudices that formerly kept the evangelical denominations too much apart from each other. His charitable spirit got the better of his former distrust of those whom he once regarded as schismatical and heretical.

Though his manner was ungraceful and his pronunciation not always precise, his impassioned earnestness overcame these defects, and enabled him to impress his audience with the emotions which thrilled his own bosom. Thus he shone, not as a star of the first magnitude, but as a luminary imparting its light to many orbs which shone around him.

As he composed his sermons with rapidity, his handwriting was scarcely legible; but the characteristics of his style were vigor and animation. There was a condensation of thought and terseness of expression which were unabating. Those who attended his preaching understood better than others the progress of his reasoning. His manner of handling subjects was familiar to them. They readily perceived the working of his mind. He never indulged in diffuseness nor in husbanding his subject, as it is called, but went directly into it, and made it luminous as he advanced. When he was told of some one who believed he had heard voices or received messages from departed friends, he preached a sermon on the calling up of Samuel by the witch of Endor, in which he refuted the whole theory of communing with spirits, and boldly asserted that no one ever returned from the invisible world but Jesus Christ, and that all statements of receiving messages from departed friends are fallacious.

During his ministry twelve new churches were organized in

the County of Bristol, and he had no little influence in the formation of most of them, and in the settlement of their pastors, who were mostly young men. Without disparaging any of his compeers, we may say that he stood eminent among them for the soundness of his doctrine and ability in contending for the true faith. He published more from the press than all the members in the two or three associations to which he successively belonged.

There were raised up in the church during his pastorate ten ministers, who were pastors of churches; eight of them were graduated at Brown University—a greater number than in any other church in the county.

When the choir fell into some difficulty, as singers are apt to, and took their seats below, and thus proclaimed their disagreement to the whole congregation, Mr. Andros made them blush by reading the account of Paul and Silas singing at midnight, and applied the subject in this manner: "Thus Paul and Silas could sing at midnight in prison, though we can have no singing at midday, while enjoying our liberty." Then Deacon Sanford rose, and in his clear voice set the tune, and the house echoed to the song.

An eminent scholar, who received his early training under his ministry, William Mason Cornell, S. T. D., editor, Boston, in one of his publications says of Mr. Andros, that he can say the same of him that Cicero does of the Poet Archias:

"As far back as my memory extends, and can recall the incidents of my boyhood, I perceive that he has been to me my guide and assistant in undertaking and pursuing the chief studies of my life."

Neither did he indulge in demonstrations against other denominations, which he considered erroneous. Every preacher must have his peculiar style and method. He aimed at imitating no one; but in his pulpit exercises appeared to forget himself, and to be absorbed in the subjects which filled his mind.

He possessed the descriptive talent in no small degree, but had very little mastery over the tender emotions, and had no great skill in the delineation of character, except the character of the natural heart. In this he excelled every one I have ever heard. He considered every man unrenewed as "dead in trespasses and sins." In describing the natural state of man, he would use expressions drawn from the word of God, nor did he think any expressions too strong to portray the evil of the natural heart. He would say that its deceitfulness cannot be fully known by us. He, however, judged tenderly and charitably of all men; and when I asked him respecting the conversion of an individual, he said he did not know men's hearts, but waited to see how they lived. He was not a sensational preacher, never sought for startling expressions or bold metaphors, but let the truth appear in its plainness and simplicity. Some have said there are no naked truths in Christianity; but that in order to be received by the intelligent or refined, they must be dressed in tasteful and eloquent language, and receive a finish and embellishment which rhetoric only can give. Without this they want the chief signature of divinity. But he thought otherwise, and never studied the gloss or drapery which the imagination may throw around such truths to make them pleasing.

He aimed to give efficiency to what he preached by having it exert its proper influence on his own mind, that with it he might impart to others the sentiments of his own soul. He never sought to set forth divine truth tricked out in the garb of an artificial rhetoric, or a prettiness of style, or in labored sentences, or with an insipid floridness. His sermons were not essays, nor were they obscure, but came from the soul in the language of strong feeling. He laid down his doctrine and illustrated it under specified heads, that his hearers might remember. Thus he touched the great springs of the soul, laying a quickening hand on our love and veneration, our hope and our joy.

Since the days of President Edwards, theological style has become more succinct and free from verbosity and a more lively, vigorous and colored style has obtained. Could the learned student peruse the writings of Mr. Andros, he would find many qualities that never can become obsolete—a clearness of expression and a singular appropriateness between the language and the thought; especially would he see the skillful arrangement or plan of his discourses, and that the main points were not lost sight of. He was eminent in his devotional exercises, especially in public.

When he settled in Berkley there was no stipulation made with him by the society that he might enjoy a vacation of a month or two in the summer to recruit his health and visit his friends abroad. When once in a few years he was absent on a journey to Connecticut, he almost invariably provided a supply for his pulpit without any expense to his people.

So strong was his habit of writing his thoughts every week that he practised it after he left the pulpit. When I called on him one day he told me he had been revolving in his mind an important subject, and had just been writing it out in a sermon which perhaps he should never preach; but it was a relief to him to write it.

He said, when his mind was low and his thoughts grovelling, it elevated him to contemplate the works of God, to reflect that this diurnal sphere, the earth, had been sent forth by him and sustained in its revolutions for thousands of years without gaining or losing a second of time; that the Eternal Father had his throne above millions of rolling worlds like this. No miracles were more convincing to him of God's almightiness than these facts, which filled him with profound admiration and adoring gratitude. Besides all, he said, to contemplate the wondrous plan of redemption which God had always had in His mind, which He had been executing by sending His Son into the world, and giving his Holy Spirit to effectuate the redemptive work, impressed him with exalted views of the divine character. Such was his flow of thought and freedom of expression in petition and praise, that he was often too long in public prayer, and as he was not weary, he was unconscious that the people were weary standing. He rarely addressed Jesus Christ in public devotion, though he spoke of him as God, and believed that "in him dwells all the fulness of the godhead bodily."

There was no studied oratory in his manner. In delivering his earnest thoughts, he sometimes clinched his hand, and would bring it nervously down upon the desk—never stretched out his arm as if conscious of doing it, or as if thinking of himself, but as if impelled by the thoughts he wished to impress on his hearers.

When preaching at a private house one evening, he touched upon the subject of prayer, and, toward the conclusion, being wrought up into a calm ecstacy, he stretched out his long arms, and with a countenance radiant with a sense of divine benevolence, cried as with the voice of a herald, "Come to the fountain of living waters; look unto Him, and be ye saved;" and so went on for some time, uttering the most startling and quickening expressions, of which some more than forty years afterwards have reminded me.

He was not a politician in the ordinary sense of the term, but a firm supporter of our national politics. It can scarcely be said he was of no party, for he advocated peace when our government was waging war against Great Britain. Though he had suffered every thing but death in the British prison ship, he saw the injustice of the war made to help France. He was fearless in exposing national wrongs, just as our pulpits during the late rebellion spake out freely and plead for national union.

During the war of 1812, he, on Fast and Thanksgiving days preached against it and against French influences. He said he rejoiced that Governor Strong withheld the troops, for if he had not, the bones of many of our citizens would be bleaching on the plains of Canada.

On Fast day it was usual to have two public discourses in the meeting house. One morning of a Fast day Mr. Andros preached a sermon well filled with political matters, the war under Madison raging, and Rev. Mace Shepard of Little Compton R. I. who was present, perceived that some of the hearers were a little irritated. In the afternoon Mr. Shepard was invited to the pulpit, and he commenced his sermon thus, "You have this morning been receiving instruction on the subject of politics, and such instruction as the Bible confirms. I shall now endeavor to clinch the nail which has been driven by the master of assemblies."

During his long ministry in the same parish, he became well known through an extensive region of the country. Hence, he was often called to attend church councils, and assist at ordinations. His judgment and advice were sought because he well understood the congregational system, and preferred it, though he was on friendly footing with all evangelical bodies. To the Lord's table he invited all in regular standing, saying this is the Lord's table, not ours, and he welcomes all his friends. He exhibited a rare example of Christian charity, and was free from that narrow-minded jealousy which confines the privileges of salvation to its own little coterie.

It is certain that he not only kept up with the times, but in many things in advance of them. This is evident from his preaching and his published writings. Yet no man was ever more strenuous for the main doctrines of oxthodoxy.

It might justly be said of him:
"With words succinct, yet full without a fault,
He said no more than just the thing he ought."

He was beneficent sometimes almost to a fault, considering his moderate income. The same kindness was shown by him to all with whom he transacted business.

In his family he was always cheerful, considerate, generous and indulgent; always praying for the absent, especially those exposed to the dangers of the sea. The proof of his good influence in his family was that his children were industrious, well educated, intelligent and upright.

He was very much affected by the death of his daughter Clarisa, who was a very amiable girl. She died of fever brought on by sitting near an open window in the meeting house. The air blew on her, and she had not courage to rise to close the window or change her seat. "It was in her bridal hour, and when fond man pronounced her bliss complete." She was as beautiful as young, and the first of his family taken from him. When her fair form was let down into the grave, he writhed and trembled as he sat in his carriage, overcome with grief. The next sabbath he preached her funeral sermon, in which he described the soul as it leaves the body and enters on immortality and the awards of eternity in such vivid colors as almost to startle some from their seats. That consolation which he had often endeavored to administer to others in a like case he now found difficult to apply to himself. Greater and better men in weeping over a fallen child have said, "Would God I had died for thee." For what so afflicts the soul, as to see one, flesh of our flesh, "the human face divine," made in God's image, covered with the clods of earth.

He was uniformly opposed to putting any confidence in dreams, and considered them unreliable. But his daughter Clarisa had a remarkable dream, which so impressed her that she told it next morning to her friends, and said she thought she should not go to her school. It was this: she would close her school in one week; would then be taken sick, and in one week more would die. This was announced to her by some one whom she saw in her dream; all which was fulfilled in every particular. After this Mr. Andros was never heard to condemn dreams, but seemed to admit that some might be worthy of consideration.

No man was more free from superstition or from belief in apparitions and spectres. yet, as he was riding home one evening and turning the corner near Mr. Abner Burt's, he said that he saw as the moon shone through the broken clouds, his wife walking a few rods before him, he knew her gait and figure and in a few minutes as he was about to speak to her, she vanished like Eurydice from Orpheus.

In argument or repartee few were equal to him. At a store he met a man whose nick-name was "Razor Ben" who thinking he would have a joke with the minister, asked him why a hog's head was called "minister's face," "Why; said Mr. Andros," it proceeds from the depravity of the heart just as the term "Razor Ben" does.

When he was criticising a sermon that had a long introduction, he said it was like making the porch larger than the house.

When he read Rev. Jacob Norton's pamphlet on Creeds which, commencing with many bland expressions, proceeded to denounce them, he said it made him think of the prophetic beast, which had horns like a lamb but spake like a dragon.

Some one observed to him how prudent he was in being able to support his large family on so small a salary, "yes," he replied, "if I can keep my chin above water, it is all I can expect."

In the westerly part of the town was a good lady who went by the name of Aunt Beck. On her premises was found a hen's egg, on which was written as if with indelible ink, this sentence, "Woe to the inhabitants of Berkly." She thought it portended some calamity, as it was a time of contention in the town, and said she would show it to the minister. As he soon came that way she brought it to him that he might interpret it. On examining it he said, it is not from any heavenly messenger, for the word Berkley is spelled wrong. This reply relieved her fear.

When Mr. Andros was asked if it was proper for a minister to marry a woman who was not a professor of religion, he said, "yes, if she is not a heathen."

When a baggage wagon loaded with tea chests was overset near the "rock house" corner and the neighbors came out to give assistance, numbers of them filled their pockets with tea from the broken chests. The next sabbath he preached a sermon from these words, "and the barbarous people showed us no small kindness," in which he showed how unkind and unjust it was to illtreat persons who have met with misfortunes. And though he named no persons, all knew to whom his discourse applied.

If there were any improprieties in the young in holding night assemblies for mirth and jollity, he was sure soon to bring out a discourse which would indirectly but plainly enough apply to the whole case, though none were arraigned or pointed out. In this indirect but faithful manner he rebuked the evil practices of the times.

When an intoxicated stranger in the gallery one sabbath began to make disturbance by climbing over from one pew to another, Judge Tobey, the warden, rose and requested the constable to put him out. After this had been done, and quiet was restored, Mr. Andros arose and said: I have for some time thought of preaching to you on intemperance, but what you have now witnessed should be equal to a whole discourse on the subject.

It was mentioned to him that some went to the tavern across the road on sabbath noon to take a drink, because they had a head ache. "Well," said he, "I should let my head ache a long time before I would do it." It has been said that all ministers and church members were formerly in the habit of taking a little, but he was never known to, either on public or private occasions.

Great deference was paid to his judgment and decision in all church and society matters. When he was coming out of the inner door of the meeting house, a young lady was introduced to him as desirous of being admitted to the communion; he took her by the hand and asked her if she could leave the vanities of the world and follow Christ. She said she thought she could. "Well," said he, "I will propound you at the close of the service."

When a young man was going to preach in a neighboring place, some one observed, he doubted whether the people would be satisfied with him. "They will not," said he, "unless he can make them believe he knows something."

He received the honorary degree of A. M. from Brown University in 1790. What President Quincy of Harvard said of William Wirt, who was never a member of any college, might as truly be said of Rev. Mr. Andros, "You are proof that a college education is not essential to every professional man." Mr. Andros was always sensitive in respect to his literary and scholarly reputation.

As he was walking home from Boston where he had been to

attend the Anniversaries, Dr. J. Codman fell in with him and learned his straitened circumstances. A few days afterwards the Doctor sent him fifty dollars. He never let the narrowness of his means distress him but said it stimulated him to preach better, and he hoped he could say with Paul, "As poor yet making many rich," and that he could say of his ministry as Goldsmith did of his Muse, "She found me poor and keeps me so." Yet he was not really poor, or involved in debt, but by his industry lived comfortably. His library was small, but what he had were standard works and were read and well understood. He highly valued Milner's Church History and said, if he had had it at the beginning of his ministry he should much more have profited by it. The bulky Commentaries he needed not, for his thorough study of the scriptures with collateral history supplied their place. He said, when he preached on some difficult points in theology, and some did not well understand them and made objection, that he had one man in his church, meaning Deacon S. who always understood them and could defend them.

When one somewhat skeptical complained to him that if he preached such doctrines as he had done his hearers would fall off, "No," said he, "they will fall off, if I do not preach them." He believed that the plain exhibition of the doctrines of the gospel was more attractive to people than to preach them partially or incompletely. Hence when he was sent as a delegate to the General Association and was appointed to preach the Associational sermon, he took two sermons with him, one somewhat philosophic and erudite, which he intended to preach before that learned body, the other plain and evangelical. But on arriving at the place, and perceiving the divines and others to be spiritual and scriptural people, he laid aside the learned sermon he had intended to preach, and delivered the other.

He was quite sensitive in regard to certain itinerant preachers who sometimes came into the outskirts of the town and held meetings. He considered that such a course led to divisions in parishes. But when Rev. James Barnaby, a Baptist, whose services were highly acceptable, came to visit his friends in his native town, Mr. Andros always invited him to his pulpit.

He had an appointment to preach at the house of Nathan French. When he arrived there Mrs. Lucy King, a woman of great memory and some prejudices gave him a text to preach from like this, "And as ye go, preach, saying the kingdom of heaven is at hand,—freely ye have received, freely give," supposing no doubt it would embarass him. But after a moment's meditation, he arose and preached an excellent sermon. Sudden occasions like that often quickened his powers of invention.

There was a time in his ministry when he dwelt much on certain points of Calvinism, but longer experience taught him that many were not by them won to the Saviour. Yet he never withheld any truth which he considered evangelical, however distasteful to prejudiced minds.

Every intelligent and sensible Christian knows that a minister who has pursued his profession for many years, preaches more from his own experience of divine truth than from books; while the beginner has not the extended views that longer study and practice will give.

The exercise of discipline in his church was strict and meant to be scriptural. In 1807 large numbers were admitted. In a few years there was a sifting out of eight or ten who were false converts. I have heard him complain that in the course of years he had had in his church almost every kind of criminal, yet it was in fact as a whole, a very spiritual and devoted church.

He was strongly opposed to the practice of members removing from one church to another for "better edification," and when some applied for letters of dismission to go and unite with a Taunton church he contended against it.

One cold sabbath morning, that his family might ride, he came walking up to the meeting house clad in a shawl, before shawls were much worn by gentlemen, and some thought it was a milled blanket. Not many days afterwards, some of the principal women came together and procured for him an excellent broadcloth cloak. He was like many talented men, somewhat negligent in his dress, and could not bear to spend much time in fitting himself out for public services.

At funerals, so tender were his sympathies, he found it difficult to control his emotions, and seemed like Euripedes in the drama when personating a man who had lost a child, he grasped the urn that contained the ashes of his own son, and poured forth such lamentations as threw the whole theater into tears. Yet no man knew better how to present the consolations of the word of God to the bereaved, for he had often been bereaved and could use the motto of the poet Virgil, "*Miser miseris succurere disco,*"—miserable myself, I learn to succor the miserable.

He lived to follow to the narrow house all the church and society who invited him to become their minister.

As he lived two miles from his meeting house he could not visit his people as he wished, but when he heard of any that were sick, old or young, he made it a point to see them, and many too who never contributed any thing for the support of the ministry. He considered it the great duty of people to attend public worship and said, "it was the chief duty of the sabbath." When a man who usually attended only in the forenoon asked him to preach on a certain text, he said he would, but perhaps it would be on some afternoon.

He had such confidence in his people and they in him that he could say anything he wished. There were but a few capable of offering prayer, or speaking in meetings to edification, not having acquired the habit in their youth. I heard him say in a religious meeting he wished those only to take a part who were capable.

He said he was always glad when he could talk to his people, and his "Lecture room talks" were always interesting.

When he was old he was still esteemed by those who knew his worth and faithfulness, as may be inferred from the following: A young minister just graduated at Andover, came home and by invitation having preached in his pulpit, a respectable lady was asked how she liked the young minister.

"Well," she said, "he preached quite well for a beginner; but, 'no one when he hath drank old wine straightway desireth the new, for he saith the old is better.'" This answer, told to the aged pastor, was quite cheering.

After serving the people in the ministry nearly fifty years he resigned, as there were some divisions that caused the calling of several councils which unhappily failed to produce general harmony. He resigned because he thought some were tired of him and desired a young pastor. But his old friends gathered round him anew, and wishing to show him some new proof of their respect, chose him representative to the General Court, in 1836.

He never left the church or the sanctuary, but always attended on the sabbath when health permitted.

After his resignation numerous ministers occupied the pulpit. Some were settled for a short time. Among those employed, I may mention the reverend gentlemen, Messrs. Ebenezer Gay, J. U. Parsons, Richardson, Rockwell, Gould, Babcock, C. Chamberlain, Smith, Lothrop, Eastman, Davis, Barney.

It may be determined by the present generation whether the settling and removing of ministers every few years, is more beneficial to a religious society than to settle a man for life, who, expecting to live and die with his people, will have time to improve and instruct them.

Not long after his resignation another altar was set up, a new church formed by advice of council, as most expedient on account of unhappy division, and disagreement, and two young ministers were employed to preach to his divided congregation. An intelligent lady expressed the sentiments of some when she said those young ministers were good men, though they had not called at her house, but she doubted whether both would fill the place of the old minister.

Installation exercises of Mr. John U. Parsons, March 14, 1838. Sermon by Rev. E. Maltby. Charge, by Rev. P. Colby. Address to the people, by Rev. E. Sanford. Prayer, by Rev. Baalis Sanford.

Mr. Parsons was born at Parsonsfield, Me. Graduated at Bowdoin College, 1828. Studied at Andover Seminary, and licensed 1831, at New York.

The last days of this excellent man were tranquil and full of hope. He knew he had not lived and labored in vain. It was a greater trial to him to resign his pulpit and lay down his profession, than resign his life and bid farewell to earth. When about eighty-seven he perceived a slight attack of paralysis, which in a small degree so affected his speech, that when he attempted to utter a word in a sentence, he uttered one not intended.

When we see a stately ship, loaded with costly merchandise, cast upon a rocky shore by the force of the waves and the tempest, a feeling of sadness comes over our minds. How much more when we see a man who has been eminent for talent and excellent deeds, on whose lips great assemblies have hung for many years, disabled and deprived of those physical and mental powers which once distinguished him,

As the Saviour ascended with outstretched arms, blessing his disciples, so did this man depart. Many have died as philosophers, but he as a Christian who had fought a good fight.

The monument raised *in memoriam* will commemorate for centuries his name and the names of his numerous family. He is worthy of such distinction. No such costly mausoleum as this rises in the town, so beautiful to the eye, so suggestive of moral greatness and earthly fame. It was erected by his affectionate children; and had it been given by the town it would have been to its honor, and a token of the gratitude which it owed him.

Yet he has left a memorial of himself worth more, and more enduring than this splendid marble, and that is, the impress of his sentiments and of divine truth, which he made during his long ministry, on the minds of his people, an impress which will endure through successive generations to the end of time.

Says Edmund Burke, " They who do not treasure up the memory of their ancestors do not deserve to be remembered by their posterity." But what shall be said of those with whom it is a matter of indifference who their ancestors were, or whether they had any.

In the first twenty-nine years of his ministry, one hundred

and thirty-four persons united with the church, and probably as many more during the remainder of his pastorate. The number of baptisms would probably equal if not exceed the admissions.

One day he baptized in the meeting-house more than fifty children. It was a May day, on a Sabbath set apart for the purpose in 1807. As the children were gathered round him, he stretched out his hands and repeated the words of Christ, "Suffer little children to come unto me." Many were moved by those emotions which cause smiles and tears at the same time, in seeing so many offered at the baptismal font. It seemed to be a scene like that when the children in the temple sang "hosanna to the Son of David." Some were infants, but many were between the ages of five and eight. They looked upon the venerable man as their father and guide. Such was the love of all for him on that memorable day.

> "Even children followed with endearing wile,
> And plucked his gown to share the good man's smile."

When he preached in Raynham the ordination sermon of Rev. E. Sanford, October 2d, 1823, he wore a clerical gown, after the ancient fashion. The audience was very large, but his voice was heard distinctly in every part of it. His subject was, "The peculiar duties of young pastors." Dr. Park, of Brown University, observed, that in preparing that discourse, he must have thought of many things, or he could not have made it so clear and forcible.

When he delivered the charge to Rev. Chester Isham, first pastor of the Trinitarian Church, Taunton, Leonard Bacon, asked who that aged man was, and being told, said he had screamed out more good sense than he had heard in the same compass for a long time.

In addressing a certain school, he described very graphically the doom of liars, and one scholar about twelve years old shed tears. When asked afterward why he was so affected, the answer was, he had never heard or read any such thing before, as he had lived a distance from religious meetings, and he supposed he had told many falsehoods. He afterwards became a good and honored citizen.

I asked Mr. Andros respecting some things, whether it were proper to perform them on the Sabbath: he said, the great and chief duty of the Sabbath was to attend public worship; hence he often had a third service on the Sabbath at five o'clock, in some part of the town.

A worthy lady died leaving an only daughter in indigent circumstances and without a home. She soon afterwards married a wealthy and excellent man. I observed to him that I wished her mother had lived longer, that she might know the success of her daughter. "O," said he. "she knows it." Hence I infer that he believed that departed friends know the circumstances of those whom they leave behind.

When a candidate for the ministry was presented to the Association for licensure and was asked by the moderator if he had in writing his articles of belief, he said he had not; but as he had received his education under Mr. Andros' preaching, he had uniformly believed what he preached from the Scriptures. On this statement the association gave him a license.

In the theories of geologists Mr. Andros had little or no belief, but considered the declarations of Moses respecting the creation as a true history. He considered the six days of creation as literal days, as they are stated to be in the command, "six days shalt thou labor," and not each an unlimited period of many millions of years as represented by Dr. John Mason Good. When this subject was discussed in the Association he showed how ridiculous it was to "dig into the earth to find proofs that Moses was mistaken in its age," and that rocks and fossils could give a better history than divine revelations, yet had he lived longer he would have modified his opinion and have seen that geological systems are reconcilable with the scriptures.

In the sermon he preached at the funeral of Miss Fanny Paul, he described heaven in very glowing colors, and towards the conclusion said, "In parting with your friends you need not say you know not where they go, or where they are, for they enter that world I have described; our sister is there; she is among the redeemed; she has seen angels; she is hearing them sing; and more than all, she beholds the face of him whom she has sought and loved, and will enjoy forever." Some on retiring said they should not fear to depart, they felt heaven to be near, they could almost look in.

When I asked him if he thought any were saved who had no knowledge of Christ or divine revelation, he said yes, no doubt if they loved God, but had no opportunity to know his Son, and had a heart to receive him if made known to them, but if when made known they rejected him, he saw not how they could be fit for heaven. He said he thought God might make men holy when they knew not by what means they were made so, just as men are often healed of diseases by remedies of which they have no knowledge.

On a slight view his life seemed hard and ascetic, but on a closer examination it would be seen to blossom continually with patience and hope, humility and tenderness. He lived for the simple performance of duty, not for show or applause, coveting neither honor or renown, and generations following will testify that for him the path of duty was the path of honor. No other profession or position in society could have made his life more worthy of respect, or more beautiful to the admirer of eminent talent. He thanked God that his incomes, lands and estates were not great, but sufficient. He has left a name like a beacon light to those who struggle in the ministry and in maintaining fellowship with heaven, a name forever fragrant, acquired in the humble labors of his profession during half a century, and that name in the archangel's book is one who loved his flock and his fellow men.

MEETING HOUSES.

The first was built about the year 1736, and stood at the south end of the "Common." It remained about sixty-one years, a plain structure without bell, steeple or blinds. It had galleries on three sides fronted with balusters turned in a lathe, and the pews were mostly surrounded with the same kind of work. When the house was taken down these frontings were sold and used for front fences to houses. Plain and rude as this house would appear now, it was equal to the style of the buildings of that day, and though warmed by no stoves, but such as women carried in, as hand or foot stoves, yet it was to the people a delightful place and on the sabbath was well filled by an attentive and devout assembly. Then newspapers were not, and books and periodicals were scarce, and from the pulpit came to the people instruction that elevated their minds, and gave them subjects of thought for days following.

The second house after long delay was built on the same spot and was dedicated November 22, 1798. The architect was Isaac Babbit, of Berkley, who built Dighton and Berkley bridge, Howland's Ferry bridge, Weir bridge, factories and other edifices. It had a tall steeple, the base of which projected several feet from the main building. a good sounding bell, a lofty pulpit, a large crowning window behind it, three aisles from the entrance doors, galleries on three sides, the orchestra opposite the pulpit, the floors were uncarpeted, the seats uncushioned. The many large windows had neither blinds nor curtains, excepting one or two after many years. There was no carpet, cushioned desk, or soft seat in the pulpit. Two pews were built for negroes in a lofty position at the corners above the stairs, though never occupied, except by John Terry, who was as much better than many below him as his seat was above them. After this house had stood over fifty years, it was thought to be out of style, unsuitable, and dangerous to the health of the people. It gave way to a third edifice more elegant, more commodious and which accommodates a large assembly. It stands on the same sacred spot where the two others stood. It has a basement story making a pleasant vestry or lecture room.

The other meeting house called the chapel was built to accommodate a new church and society, which were seceders from the first society. They were organized in a regular way by a council who deemed it advisable on account of divisions which had arisen. It has been found that a greater number of people attend public worship on the sabbath in the two houses than did before in one. The churches have for some time been in good fellowship. Their first pastor was the Rev. Lucius R. Eastman, Amherst, 1833. Their present pastor is Rev. James A. Robarts, formerly of New Bedford, and previously pastor of a dissenting church, London.

The two first meeting houses were used for town meetings, and the town often raised money for repairs on them. But when the third house was built, the town, by law and decision of courts, surrendered this privilege.

TOPOGRAPHY.

This town is oblong in shape, extending about seven miles along the east side of Taunton river, terminating at the south in a cape called Assonet Neck which lies between Assonet river and the Taunton. At the extreme point of this neck is Conspiracy Island, so called probably from a conspiracy formed by King Philip against the first settlers. The farms bordering on the river are rich and productive, containing Burt's meadows, so-called, and numerous salt meadows at the south. The town is mostly level, but embraces several hills, as Ape's hill at the north, Skunk's hill at the east, and Philip Hathaway's hill near the centre. The easterly part borders on the Cotley river, a small mill stream tributary to the Taunton; through this part runs the railway to New Bedford.

In the centre of the town is a public park or "common" containing about nine acres in the form of a triangle, partly surrounded with elms. There are six roads or highways radiating from the common into the various parts of the town; surrounding it are twelve fine dwelling houses, among them are two churches and a school house. The town hall stands near the centre. General musters used to be held here, and in 1803 a brigade comprising the militia of the county encamped here under command of Brigadier Gen. James Williams, of Taunton, father of Chief Justice J. M. Williams, L.L.D. Near the centre of this park once stood a windmill for grinding grain, granted by the town to be built by S. Tobey, Esq., in 1787; but about 1805 it was removed, having become old and dangerous. Scarcely any town in the county can show so pleasant a centre as this. It might be made still more pleasant and inviting by placing more trees and shrubbery on the borders of the roads that environ it.

As ancient Sparta consisted of five towns, so this town may be considered as containing five villages. The north is called the Burt neighborhood, in which are numerous families of that name, of considerable wealth. Farming, mechanical business, and trade have flourished there.

On the river is the Bridge village, near where Dighton and Berkley bridge stood, which was built in 1806, and removed about 1850, having become defective, and deemed an obstruction to navigation. This village contains many enterprising people, farmers, mechanics, navigators, ship builders, traders and fishermen.

The next village further down the river is Assonet neck, made up mostly of enterprising farmers, who excel in raising fat cattle and other domestic animals. Levi Pierce, a bachelor, owned a large farm at the extreme end of the cape. He began with nothing, but by industry and parsimony acquired a good property. He had only his sister, for some years, to guide his hermitage, and after her death was alone except that he had numerous cattle and swine, the latter taking the milk of his cows, for he could find no one to manage a dairy. As he could not afford the expense of a new roof for his shanty, he usually lodged in his barn when it rained. In going any distance he would carry his shoes in his hands rather than on his feet, and when he wore them would put leaves in them to save the expense of stockings. When I visited him I asked him for his almanac; he said he had none, nor any book in the house as he was unable to read. I mentioned to him that as he had no near relatives, he could leave his property to the town for educational purposes, or to some benevolent society. He said he thought strangers were as good to him as his own relatives, who seemed to want what he had. He said he made his first earnings by collecting oyster shells in a small boat or lighter, and carrying them about fifteen miles up the river to the furnaces in Raynham, where they were used in fusing iron.

The fourth village is in the easterly part of the town, embracing some dozen houses, situated amid verdant meadows and forests of pine, oak, cedar, walnut and birch, which once were not thought valuable, but now are considered the best of property.

The centre village has been already sufficiently described. Near the meeting house was a pound with high walls, about two rods square, in which mischievous or stray cattle might be confined according to law. In the gate, at or near the bottom, were stocks in which the authorities might confine the feet of the refractory; but none ever had that distinction. There are now one hundred and twenty-two dwelling houses in the town.

NAVIGATORS.

In this town a large number have been employed in the commercial marine, some of whom I may mention. Capt. John Sanford, son of John, and grandson of John, the first settler of that name in Taunton, sailed mostly to the West Indies. My father, his cousin, went with him one voyage. His voyages were successful. He owned two or three farms in the southerly part of the town. He died in 1780, leaving three daughters, Sophia, who married Rev. Thomas Andros; Esther, who married Capt. John Dillingham, and Sarah, who married Mr. Seth Winslow, and dying left one daughter, Sally, who married Capt. Daniel Burt; and their only daughter, Sarah Ann, married the late Henry H. Fox, of Taunton. One of whose sons, William H. Fox, Esq., is Judge of the Municipal Court, Taunton.

Capt. Barnabas Crane was an intelligent and distinguished

From sundry old documents lately exhumed by Rev. M. Blake, D.D., of Taunton, it is ascertained when ship building began on this river.

August 12, 1694, in the reign of William and Mary, Thomas Hunt, of London, contracted with one Greenfell Hanover, shipwright, to come to New England for the purpose of building vessels After spending some time in the business at Boston, Mr. Hanover came to Taunton to build a vessel for a Mr. Coram, for which he was to receive, having all materials furnished him, the sum of £41 current money of New England. This was the first of the thousands of vessels that have plied by sailing, rowing or steaming on the Taunton river. The name, career, and final anchorage of this vessel, says Dr. Blake, are unknown. It was completed August 30, 1698, and was fifty-four feet keel and twenty feet beam.

navigator. He removed to Dighton, then to Ohio, where he settled with his sons on a fine plantation.

Capt. Ephraim French, sen., was by long experience better acquainted with the Taunton river and the southern coast than any other man. He taught numerous young men the art of navigation, from a treatise by John H. Moore.

Capt. Jabez Fox followed the sea some years, and settled on a farm near Assonet neck. Capt. Enoch Tobey made foreign voyages in his father's ships, often to Liverpool, and was some time successful, but died early. His brother, Silas, graduate of Brown University, made voyages to Havana, where he suddenly died of fever. He had married a daughter of Dr. Fuller, of Kingston, a physician. He left one son, Hon. Edward S. Tobey, of Boston, president of the Board of Trade, member of numberless benevolent associations, a merchant possessed of immense wealth.

Capt. Seth Burt and his brother, Daniel, made trips to the Carolinas. In a storm they were both lost, and all on board with them, their vessel being shallow and not well ballasted.

Capt. Albert French has for years followed the southern trade, in his own vessels, and always with satisfactory results.

The sons of Rev. Thomas Andros, Milton, William, Thomas, Benedict and Kendrick, have been among the boldest and most successful navigators from any of our ports or cities. They were well educated, loved the seas, and commanded some of the largest ships that sailed out of Providence or New York. They rarely met with losses. William, however, in entering the North sea to go to Hamburg, encountering one of those tempests which often arise there, lost both vessel and cargo. After coming home to New York the owners found no fault with him, but gave him command of another ship. He lost his life some years after, at Valparaiso. Thomas and Benedict, after a long life at sea, died at home.

Daniel Sanford, son of Deacon George, bid fair to become a courageous and able navigator. He made several foreign voyages; was then pilot of a steam boat plying between Providence and New York, Capt. Comstock, commander, and by some accident was thrown overboard in the night, and was drowned.

Jonathan Crane, brother of Col. A. Crane, followed the southern trade for some years, and at length contracting the southern fever, came home and died. He was a most amiable young man, a distinguished singer, and played the flute in the choir on the sabbath.

Capt. John Briggs, son of John, the mason, was a bold hardy master of a whale ship, made profitable voyages of three years in the Pacific ocean; would stand on the bow of a tossing boat to hurl the harpoon, courage supplied the want of knowledge.

Numerous vessels of various burthen have been built in this town. Judge Tobey built one in 1806 called a ship, it having three masts, which the writer saw launched in presence of hundreds of people. Henry Crane built several schooners near his house at the Bridge village. Ephraim French, senior, usually built every winter a sloop to sell. Others were built at Burt's wharf. Barzillai Hathaway built vessels and chartered them. About the year 1800 a sloop was built a little east of Timothy's Hollow, and drawn on trucks over the prairie to the river, a distance of about a mile. I remember seeing the deep tracks the trucks made.

GROCERS AND TRADERS.

Of these there were not many, because of the vicinage of Taunton, the head of navigation. Hon. S. Tobey and son traded in dry goods, about fifty years, and after them Abiel Crane, who at length removed his store to Taunton, (Weir). Simeon Burt traded in West India goods, and imported them in his own vessels. Luther Crane kept a store at the Bridge village, and after him Ephraim French, jr., who was also Town Clerk, and died in middle life. These stores, excepting the last, dealt in ardent spirits: the temperance reformation not having arisen, and most people of that time thinking that laborers needed stimulants. But no town for the last twenty years has been more free from their destructive influence. There were two taverns perhaps down to the year 1825. One was kept by Capt. Samuel French, sen.; the other, near the meeting-house, was kept by Ezra Briggs. These inns were thought essential, as before the railways were laid, three or four stages a day used to pass between Taunton and Fall River, and there was much travelling in other vehicles. A post office was not opened in this town till about 1824.

EDUCATION.

Soon after the town was organized schools were opened. One teacher only was employed, Roland Gavin, an Englishman, who received a stated salary from the treasury, about £16 per year, worth perhaps eighty-six dollars.

His school was migratory, that is, it was kept about two months at a place and in rotation, at several localities in the course of a year or two, in houses or rooms that now would be thought mere shanties, yet in general they corresponded well with other buildings.

Master Gavin never performed manual labor but devoted himself wholly to his profession. I have seen some who were his pupils. His reputation for learning was something like that of Goldsmith's school-master in the "Deserted Village."

He employed himself chiefly in teaching reading, writing, and ciphering. He would write the problem for the scholar in his manuscript book, and the pupil when he had solved it would write the solution under the question.

He also taught young men the art of navigation, for which he had an extra fee of two dollars.

As for geographies and grammars, there were none. Dillworth's was the first spelling book, then Webster's, then Abner Alden's, which had a long run, and few have improved upon it.

The first book on geography used in schools, was that of Rev. J. Morse, D. D., of Charlestown, the father of Professor Morse, the telegraph inventor; and it was used only as a reading book by the first class. After a while Blake's and Cumming's geographies came in vogue, from which lessons for recital were learned.

The first grammar was Alexander's, introduced by Joseph Sanford, in this and the neighboring towns where he taught.

Afterwards Webster's or Gurney's, then Murray's, which was used together with his English Reader, for many years. Soon after the Revolution the school district system was originated, seven schools were established, but money enough could not be raised to maintain each more than ten weeks in the winter, and the summer school, if any, was supported by contributions in part. Yet learning increased in the town. No child grew up not a good reader or writer. The less their means, the parents made greater efforts. Penmanship was more cultivated then than now, and orthography was so diligently pursued that many scholars before leaving school could spell every word in Webster's or Alden's spelling book.

The minister was required by law to examine and license teachers, and together with a committee to visit schools, gratis, as often as desirable.

After a while a number of eminent teachers was raised up in the town. Capt. Joseph Sanford commenced soon after the Revolutionary War, in which he had served over two years, and taught thirty-two winters in succession. He was superior in mathematics, algebra, navigation, and in all school studies of that day. The arithmetics he used were by Ward, Walch, Pike, Adams, Dabol, Temple, and the School Master's Assistant, which were more intricate than the later books of the kind.

Col. Adoniram Crane was an eminent teacher, who, however, used great severity in discipline, and which tended rather to harden than soften the rough spirits he had to deal with.

There were other teachers too numerous to mention; in the Sanford family, six or eight, in the Benj. Crane family as many more. These and others took great pride in qualifying themselves for their office. Some attended the academy at Taunton, then under the instruction of Rev. S. Dogget, the first preceptor, who had a great influence in raising the standard of education.

This town has steadily increased the appropriations for schools, though the population has somewhat diminished. In 1858 the population was 924, the appropriation for schools was $750, the valuation $261,405, the school districts seven, number of scholars 238. But in 1870 the population was 888, the valuation $316,002, number of schools six, number of scholars 178. But the appropriation for schools was $1.000. Thus it appears that though population diminished, the appropriation for schools in twelve years increased $250, allowing to each child for his education per year, $5.62, which compares well with towns of greater wealth.

A literary society was formed in 1810, which posessed Rees' Encyclopædia in twenty volumes, and other learned works, which were much read by the people generally.

PERSONS WHO RECEIVED A COLLEGE EDUCATION, OR WHAT WAS EQUIVALENT.

Alvan Tobey, B. U. 1799, pastor, N. H., died..........1810.
Silas Tobey. B. U. 1804, died........................1817.
James Barnaby, B. U. 1809, pastor, Harwich.
James Sandford, B. U. 1812, pastor Fabius, N. Y., died..1865.
John Sanford, B. U. 1812, pastor, South Dennis, died...1866.
Enoch Sanford, B. U. 1820, pastor, Raynham.
Silas Axtel Crane, B. U. 1823, S. T. D. 1855, pastor, E. Greenwich.
Baalis Sanford, B. U. 1823, pastor, E. Bridgewater.
George Hathaway. B. U. 1824, teacher at the South.
William Mason Cornell, B. U. 1827, pastor, Quincy, M. D. L L. D.
Daniel Crane Burt, B. U. 1828, pastor, Acushnet.
Frederic Andros, M. D. at B. U., two years, never graduated.
Benjamin Crane, B. U. two years, an eminent teacher.
Thomas Tobey Richmond, studied with Rev. A. Cobb, Westville, Taunton, and settled with him, pastor.
Richard Salter Storrs Andros, editor in New Bedford, then clerk of Secretary of State, then of Collector of Customs, Boston, then Deputy Collector, President of Insurance Company, State Street, Boston; appointed by Government in 1865, to establish Custom houses at the South. He died at middle age, in 1868, greatly lamented, and was buried near the Park in the family enclosure.

Levi French was a man of general knowledge, though not a college graduate, instructed young men in fitting for college, was pastor at New Salem. He received a degree of A. M. from Brown University, in 1825.

Milton Andros, youngest son of Rev. T. Andros, was a jurist, and Assistant District Attorney of the U.'S. at Boston.

Col. Alexander Baxter Crane, Amherst College, 1854, lawyer, N. Y. City.

Edward Crane, Amherst College, 1854, M. D., Paris, France.

Philip Chester Porter, Amherst College, 1855.

PHYSICIANS.

Jesse Bullock, M. D., who resided in Freetown, had a large practice in this town about the beginning of the present century. Being a justice of the peace, he sometimes solemnized marriages.

William Carpenter, M. D., was much employed in this town, though he resided on the borders of Freetown. He was eminent as a temperance man and fought successfully, by his addresses in public and private, against the plague of drunkness.

Fuller, M. D., of Kingston, was settled for a while at the Centre, and had he lived, would have succeeded in his profession.

Amos Allen, M. D., who graduated at B. U., 1804, studied medicine with Dr. Miller, of Franklin, was practicing physician in this town many years, and excelled as a surgeon. He at length removed to East Taunton.

Shadrach Hathaway, M. D., a native of this town, has for some years been successfully employed here and in Freetown as an intelligent physician. Dr. Job Godfrey and his son, Jonas Godfrey, B. U., 1793, of Taunton, were for many years the celebrated and acceptable physicians of this region.

Dr. Samuel Robinson, a distinguished geologist, born in Attleborough, March, 1783, studied medicine with the celebrated Dr. Nathan Smith, professor in Dartmouth College, and came to this town in 1805, and commenced practice, but he remained here only one year. He then moved to a town near

Elizabeth City, N. C., where he practiced twenty years, and became a distinguished physician and surgeon. An anecdote related of him shows him to have been a benevolent man. The leg of a poor man required amputation, and a surgeon could not be obtained for want of sufficient compensation. Dr. Robinson hearing of the circumstance, travelled many miles, and performed the operation without hope of any recompense. The wife of the poor man afterwards having twins, and both sons, named one of them Samuel, and the other Robinson.

JUSTICES OF THE PEACE.

Hon. Samuel Tobey was Justice of the Peace and Senator of the Commonwealth, and at length one of the judges of the Court of Common Pleas. He was the third child of Rev. Samuel Tobey, the first minister of the town, and stood high as a man of learning. sound judgment, and extensive influence. His presence was impressive and commanding. No one in the town was looked upon for fifty years with more respect and reverence. The wicked stood in fear of him, but the good loved him, because his influence was exerted for the improvement and welfare of all.

When the second meeting house was to be built and there was but one bank in the county, and money was hard to be obtained, and the people knew not how to bear the expense, he made them believe they could do it; sent for freestone to Connecticut for the foundation, and led on in procuring materials, and the house was built.

His pastor in the discourse at his funeral says of him: "Could all his virtues be enumerated and set in a just light, his example might long serve to put vice and meanness to the blush and to gui le and encourage those who aim to do well. I should be wanting in gratitude did I not honor him as one of my most generous, faithful, persevering friends. That he was a man eminent for a disinterested public spirit all must testify who knew him. He took a deep interest in the welfare of his native town. But he was not one of those contracted minds who view the interests of their town or parish as tantamount to all others. Being convinced of the justice and utility of a measure, he pursued it with a zeal and firmness that no opposition or temporary ill-success could conquer. To this quality is owing his success in enterprises deeply involving the welfare of the town. The general prosperity of the nation and the honor of the government under which he lived, being objects still of greater magnitude, more deeply engaged his benevolent wishes and exertions.

"He was honored with various posts in public life from the dawn of the Revolution till age and infirmity admonished him of the necessity of retirement. Yet he never was an office-seeker, he knew not how meanly to stoop to court the suffrage of the people. In the days of his greatest prosperity he affected no luxurious or splendid style of living, yet no man ever made his friends more welcome to his house or appeared more delighted, if they were rendered comfortable by his hospitality. And even in his pecuniary embarassments he did not cease to be liberal."

Apollos Tobey was Justice of the Peace and sometimes had criminals before him. He was appointed judge of the Court of Sessions, whose business was something like the present duties of County Commissioner, to grant licenses to innholders and regulate county affairs. He removed to New Bedford, and for several years was employed constantly in justice business.

Simeon Burt was a justice, but had few occasions to exercise the functions of his office, so peaceful were the times, and the people who held the laws in high respect. Simeon Chase was an upright justice, a carpenter by trade, an exemplary man, who had the confidence of all who knew him.

Ephraim French, another justice, who afterwards held other offices in the town, and dying early, was much lamented.

Barzillai Crane, Justice of the Peace, was eminent for his integrity and uprightness. As he had large means, he made use of them for the good of others.

Levi French was another Justice of the Peace who well understood town laws. He was a surveyor and settled estates. His knowledge of statutes concerning town matters was much invoked, and frequently saved to the town the expense of obtaining legal opinions.

Alpheus Sanford, a Justice of the Peace and one of the six sons of Joseph Sanford, lived in this town till 1887, then moved to Taunton, represented that town in the General Court in 1844. He excelled in building, selling and renting houses.

William Babbit, a Justice and Selectman, is prominent in the business of the town.

MECHANICS.

With this honorable class the town has been well furnished especially if we include manufacturers and ship builders. The first mason, who built many grotesque and bulky chimneys was John Sandford, who lived here as early as 1713 on a large and rough plantation a mile east of the Common. From him five generations have descended, though but few of that name now live in the town.

John Briggs was a mason, and performed the mason work on the second meeting house and in payment took a pew which he usually occupied on the sabbath.

Joseph Sanford learned the trade of him and pursued it mostly in Taunton. Three of his six sons learned and followed the business till about the age of eighteen.

Of carpenters the number was greater. Elkanah Babbit was a noted builder of houses. He lived on a good farm a little south of the meeting house. His son Isaac as mentioned above was a celebrated and intelligent workman. He settled in Dighton. Two other sons, Warren and Benjamin, were skilled workmen, but after a while removed from town.

Simeon Chase built the fine house of the late Barzillai Crane, and many others. Alpheus Sanford built the town hall. Samuel Phillips and his brother Reuben, Baalis Phillips and John Newhall were builders of houses.

The principal ship builders were Henry Crane, Ephraim French, Nehemiah Newell, Thomas Burt with numberless others in their employment.

Abner Burt, senior, was a saddler and harness maker for more than fifty years, when saddles and pillions were in great demand. He lived to a great age. His two sons Shadrach and Dean were hatters and carried on the manufacture for many years. Dean was deputy Sheriff more than a quarter of of a century, to old age and died in office.

Of shoe makers there were many. George Sanford, one of the best was a cordwainer, that is sewed with thread. Enoch Babbit was an excellent boot maker. The early custom of shoemakers was to go once or twice a year to families and make or mend as the family required out of materials on hand, in the same manner as tailoresses circulated through the neighborhood; there were no shoe stores in the country villages.

Those who slaughtered animals sent the hides to the tanner, and meat enough to pay for tanning. John Terry was a noted shoemaker and removed to Fall River.

Tisdale Porter who lived a little north of the meeting house was an ingenious blacksmith, made bolts and other iron work for ships; he was from Freetown and married a daughter of Hon. S. Tobey. Seth Burt was architect of Winslow church, Taunton. John Perkins and William S. Crane were good blacksmiths at the Bridge village.

Celia Atwood deserves to be mentioned here, a tailoress more than fifty years, and extensively useful through the town.

FISHERIES.

These have ever been of considerable annual profit to the town, which like other towns on the river has had the privilege of running two seines four days in a week for a certain number of weeks. A fishing privilege for the season has usually been sold for $250 or $300. But so much has the river been seined and obstructed from Fall River to Middleboro, that the herring have diminished, and the shad nearly ceased to run. Legislation to regulate these fisheries has not been satisfactory to all. At the southerly part of the town are beds of clams and oysters.

THE ALMS HOUSE

does not possess many occupants since the day of grogshops. The number has been gradually diminishing. Those who have been unfortunate, by loss of property or health, are received and cared for so well that one aged inmate said it was called the poor house, but she called it the rich house. It was said in the first half century after the settlement of the town that there were no drunkards, and only one man maintained by the towns and that was the minister.

Mr. N. Gilbert Townsend has had the charge of this establishment for many years.

The annual cost of supporting the poor is about six hundred dollars. The Alms House cost $3500, stock $1500, salary of the warden $150 yearly. In 1774, the poor were vendued to the lowest bidder at about four shillings a week each.

SEVERAL LADIES OF THIS TOWN

married educated men and persons of distinction from abroad. Daughters of Simeon Burt: Abigail married in 1810, Rev. James Barnaby, pastor, Harwich; Polly married William Carpenter M. D. of Freetown; and Clarissa married Mr. Peleg Gray, a grocer of New York.

Polly, daughter of Stephen Burt, married Amos Allen M. D. a physician of this town and East Taunton.

Daughters of Rev. Samuel Tobey: Bathsheba married Deacon Gideon Babbit, of Dighton; Achsah married Roger French of Berkley, and of Barnard, Vt.

Daughters of Hon. Samuel Tobey: Bathsheba married Rev. Abraham Gushee, pastor Dighton for fifty seven years; Peddy married Thomas Richmond M. D. of Dartmouth.

Abigail, daughter of Thomas Briggs, married William Cornell M. D. father of Rev. William M. Cornell L. L. D., M. D., editor, Boston.

Eleanor, daughter of James Macomber, married Capt. Joseph Sanford.

Sally, daughter of Ebenezer Paul, married, as his fifth wife, Capt. Jabez Fox, a navigator and importer.

Hannah, daughter of Abel Crane, married Apollos Tobey Esq., merchant, and for many years representative to General Court.

Experience, daughter of Christopher Paul, Sen., married Hon. Samuel Tobey, Senator and Judge of Court of Common Pleas.

Clarissa, daughter of D. Dean, married Col. Adoniram Crane, an eminent singer and teacher.

Emma T, daughter of Tisdale Porter, married, 1829, Abiel B. Crane Esq. merchant.

Caroline, daughter of Benjamin Crane, married Hon. George P. Marsh, Ambassador from our Government to Greece, and also to Italy.

Betsy, grand-daughter and adopted daughter of Hon. Samuel Tobey, married Joseph Hathaway, agriculturist.

Jerusha, daughter of Ezra Chase, married Philip French.

Rebecca Porter, daughter of Abiel B. Crane, married, 1870, Rev. Lucius R. Eastman, Jr., of Somerville.

Polly, daughter of Elisha Crane, married Deputy Sheriff Dean Burt.

Daughters of Apollos Tobey Esq. : Eliza married Deacon Barzillai Crane Esq., a man of large property ; Caroline Amelia, married Mr. Abel B. Sanford of Philadelphia.

Daughters of Dean Burt : Abby, married Rev. Baalis Sanford of East Bridgewater, pastor; Rowena, married Hon. Rodney French, Mayor of New Bedford.

Lora, daughter of Ezra Chase, married Joseph Tisdale, son of Hon. Joseph Tisdale, Senator.

Hopestill, daughter of Elkanah Babbit, married George Sanford, Jr.

Betsy, daughter of Abel Crane, married Rev. Levi Lankton of Alstead, N. H.

Sophia, d. of Capt. Christopher Paul, m. Benjamin Crane, son of Benjamin, an eminent scholar and teacher, who was member of Brown University two years and failed in health.

Daughters of Rev. Thomas Andros : Lydia married Capt. John Dean, of Freetown,

Priscilla Deane, married, 1827, Smith Winslow of Fall River,

Mary, married William Babbit, manufacturer,

Sarah, married Mr. George F. Butters, horticulturist, Newton.

Sarah Hastings Fox, adopted daughter of Shadrach Burt, married Thomas C. Dean, merchant and agriculturist.

Sally, d. of Seth Winslow m. Capt. Daniel Burt, 1814.

Daughters of Capt. Joseph Sanford: Eleanor, married Abner Pitts, of Taunton, jeweler; Mary, married Capt. Theophilus Nickerson, of South Dennis.

Rebecca, d. of Tisdale Porter, married Samuel Newhall.

Daughters of Dea. Barzillai Crane: Susan Whitmarsh, m. Samuel Breck, a lawyer, now of Bridgewater, graduate of Harvard, 1831; Irene Lazel, married Thomas C. Nichols M. D. of Freetown.

Sophia, daughter of Capt. John Dean and his wife Sally, daughter of John and Esther (Sanford) Dillingham, married James Lothrop, of Raynham, a well-known singer and musician.

MUSIC.

The first society early took measures to cultivate good singing. John Paul was appointed chorister and tuner of psalms Jan. 25, 1737. The class of tunes at first used was that to which Mear, St. Martin's and Old Hundred belonged. Then came Billings' shrill fleeting tunes which had a long run. Some think his class of tunes wrought a great improvement and agreeable variety, but they have long since been superseded by the harmonious and devotional hymns of the present day. June 3, 1773, the church voted that Nathaniel Haskins and Simeon Burt should assist Shadrach Burt in leading the psalm.

Dr. Isaac Watt's psalms and hymns began to be used in 1788, and Azael Hathaway and James Babbit were chosen choristers.

Nov. 3, 1823, it was voted by the church that Henry Crane be second chorister,—Dea. George Sanford being appointed to lead when the church observe the communion, and the choir join with the church. Also that Col. Adoniram Crane be chief chorister and that it be left to him to say who shall lead when he is absent. He was a noted singer for about thirty years, was president of the Beethoven Society, which was composed of the best singers of several towns. He sung perhaps for ten years in the second Con'l Church of this town. Dea. G. Sanford taught singing schools, and Col. Crane succeeded him many winters. Stringed instruments were long used.

OFFICERS OF THE FIRST CHURCH.
Ruling Elders.
Daniel Axtell............1750   Jacob French..........1750
John Paul...............1764   Ebenezer Crane........1789

Dec. 23. 1798, Barzillai Hathaway was chosen as agent to manage the funds of the church.

Deacons.
Gershom Crane..............1737   Daniel Axtell..........1737
Jacob French............1748   John Paul..............1748
Samuel Tubbs...........1764   Ebenezer Crane.........1764
Ebenezer Winslow.......1789   Samuel Tobey...........1789
George Sanford..........1807   Luther Crane..........1807
Tisdale Briggs...........1820   Barzillai Crane.........1837
Thomas C. Dean.........1847   James Hathaway.......1847

CHURCH DISCIPLINE.

Jany. 25, 1737. The church met and voted that liberty should be granted to persons to be admitted to the church with a relation or without as they may see their way clear.

Jany. 7, 1749. At a church meeting the following vote was passed: That if any of the brethren or children of the church should allow of frolicking in their houses, or go abroad to frolick in any other house, they should be deemed offending. That if any of the church should neglect to attend at church meetings without satisfactory reasons given, they should be deemed offending.

That if any of the church should invite into their house any of the separate Baptist teachers to preach, or follow them abroad, they should be deemed offending.

July 25, 1750. Daniel Axtell and Jacob French were ordained as ruling elders. The ordaining services were performed by delegates from the churches in Rochester and Freetown. The church usually held a lecture monthly. When one had fallen into sin and was restored, he was required to make confession, and ask forgivness before the congregation on the sabbath.

Feb. 16, 1762. Voted to inquire into the reason of Brother Pickens for his neglecting special ordinances, and also for his attending on Mr. Hind's ministry, who is an anabaptist. Mr. Pickens, reasons were that he did not profit by Mr. Turner's ministry, and the church voted that they were not satisfied with his reasons.

Feb. 29, 1816. Voted that Brother Elijah French be admonished not to attend the meetings of heretical sectarian preachers. He being present received the admonition and promised amendment. This aged brother was a very pious man, and being hard of hearing was fond of meetings at dwelling houses.

Voted also, that Mrs. Polly Hathaway be admonished for the same disorderly conduct, as also for absenting herself from the communions, and attending a seperate and opposition meeting, and for holding heretical opinions of Elias Smith. She being present gave some encouragement of reformation and four months were given her to consider and reform in respect to those charges.

It is a question whether the venerable pastor was not too rigid in some acts of church discipline. These are barely specimens; numerous other instances of little importance are recorded in an almost illegible handwriting.

THE MINISTERIAL TAX.

This tax was assessed on the inhabitants, like other taxes, according to law. It was opposed by those who did not worship with the First Society. One man had his horse distrained for non-payment of a small ministerial tax, but afterwards it was given up as being exempt from such seizure. Another man, Zephaniah Jones, was taken by warrant, and lodged in jail for refusal to pay such tax, but some friend soon released him. It was soon seen that this mode of compelling men to support the ministry was impolitic, and not necessary for the maintenance of the Church. Hence, in 1820, the law of the State was repealed, and the voluntary system of supporting the ministry henceforth obtained.

1776.

This town was well represented in the army of the Revolution, though the population and means were small. Rev. Thomas Andros as stated above, was a soldier in the Continental army. Only a few others am I able to give.

Ezra Chase enlisted in the army of Rhode Island, and being wounded in a sham fight drew a pension from that State, payable semi-annually so long as he lived. He resided on a farm in the easterly part of the town, and his nine chidren, five sons and four daughters, have long been dead.

Josiah Macomber, son of James, was in the Continental army over two years. After the war he became *non compos mentis*, and received a pension from 1818, by his guardian.

Joseph Sanford at the age of eighteen, entered the army, served at South Boston and Dorchester Heights, also in Providence, in all about two years; drew a pension from 1818 to the time of his death, excepting a few years when it was withheld from those whose income was more than two hundred dollars a year, and after his decease it was paid to his widow by act of Congress allowing it to soldiers' widows married previous to the year 1795. He was the son of George Sanford, Sen., who was in 1756 a lieutenant in the army under command of the British General Lord Loudoun, and marched against the French at Crown Point and Ticonderoga. This was the "French War," which resulted in the conquest of Canada by the British and American forces. Lieut. Sanford was the youngest child of John Sandford and his wife Abigail, daughter of Samuel Pitts.

Samuel Paul, William Evans, and Paul Briggs, were soldiers of the Revolution and drew pensions.

Colonel John Hathaway, father of Barzillai, commanded a regiment in the war, was eminent for his patriotism, had full confidence in the success of our arms, and when there was no chaplain would pray on horseback at the head of his command.

In 1774 the town voted that the resolves of the Continental Congress be strictly adhered to in every particular, and John Hathaway and others were a committee to see that these resolves were regarded by the people. 1775. Voted that the militia train half a day in a week, and be allowed one shilling; that each minute man have five dollars as a bounty if called into the service of his country.

July 22, 1776. Voted to raise £75 10s., as an additional bounty allowed to the soldiers bound to New York, and that volunteer and drafted soldiers be exempt from paying any part of it.

Feb., 1777. Voted to choose militia officers; to hire our quota required for the Continental army, and to give each soldier ten pounds additional to what is given by the General Court. They were to enlist for three years.

Nov. 24. Voted £234 to be assessed to pay soldier's bounty. Feb., 17 78. Voted £620 to pay Continental soldiers. In 1778, voted £154 12s., for soldiers. Voted £1,320 19s. to pay soldiers hired by the town. Sixty-four soldiers at different times serving for three months in the army were allowed from three to ten pounds each.

After Independence, the military spirit was dominant. The law required trainings in May, and muster in the autumn annually. All able-bodied men between the ages of eighteen and forty-five, were required to attend at a given time and place, equiped with gun, bayonet, knapsack, cartouch box, and some twenty rounds of powder and ball. For absence without legal excuse two dollars was the fine. Every town was required by law to have a powder house with a certain amount of powder and ammunition to be ready for invasion or war.

The captain and other officers of the militia wore uniforms consisting of a military hat with feathers; red-faced coats, with epauletts of silver fringes; two-edged sword, or cutlass, with silver hilt, and spontoon.

Abner Burt, Jr., was adjutant many years. Among the captains were Samuel French, Sen., and his son, the Senator, Joseph Sanford, Christopher Paul, 2d., Freeman Briggs, Giles G. Chase, who in the war of 1812, marched his company to New Bedford, to defend the coast against the incursions of the British. Other captains were Nathaniel Staples, Nathaniel Townsend, and Daniel Burt. Colonel Joseph Sanford, Jr., who died in 1827, at New York City, resided at Oswego, N. Y. He was the son of Captain Joseph Sanford, of this town.

CEMETERIES.

One of these is near the Park and contains the graves of those who first settled the town. Changing a few words we may apply to them a stanza from Gray's Elegy:

> "Here rest their heads upon the lap of earth,
> Brave men to fortune and to fame unknown,
> Fair science frowned not on their humble birth,
> Nor melancholy marked them for its own."

They were as brave and self-denying men as settled any part of the country. It was not till within the last fifty years that marble could be generally obtained. The ancient graves have the blue stone which was prepared by Dea. Ebenezer Winslow, the only sculptor or stone-cutter in town, and not very skillful. The letters are cut so shallow as to be nearly obliterated. But in later years great improvements have been made in commemorating the departed. This is proof of increased taste in the people, and their respect for deceased friends. Several family squares are finely enclosed and adorned.

The two first pastors are buried here. The grave of the Rev. Mr. Toby will soon be honored by an appropriate monument to be erected by his descendants.

Another cemetery is situated in the lower part of the town in the vicinity of Assonet Neck. Some of the earliest settlers of Freetown and Taunton, were buried here; including families of Axtel, Briggs, Burt, Crane, Paul, and Winslow. This cemetery is well enclosed and presents a pleasing aspect

BY REASON OF STRENGTH FOUR SCORE.

James Macomber, died December 31, 1803, aged 88 years.
Rachel Drake, his wife, died December 1, 1809, aged 83 years.
Lieut. George Sanford, died February 19, 1820, aged 96 years.
Sarah Sanford, his daughter, died Jan., 1845, aged 82 years.
Bernice Crane, died November, 1830, aged 86 years.
Joanna Axtel, his wife, died May 5, 1846, aged one hundred years, one month and fifteen days.

Eleanor Macomber, widow of Capt. Joseph Sanford, died August 12, 1845, aged 82 years.

Rev. Thomas Andros, son of Benjamin Andros, died Dec. 30, 1845, aged 86 years.

SELECTMEN

from the organization of the town. The year is given in which they were elected: some served several years, having been re-elected.

Joseph Burt, John Paul, Benaiah Babbit,	1735
Samuel Thresher, Elkanah Babbit,	1736
Joseph Burt, Thomas Hathaway,	1737
John French, Benaiah Paul, Ephraim Allen,	1740
Abial Atwood, Christopher Paul, Ebenezer Winslow,	1742
Gershom Crane, Joseph Burt,	1747
Samuel Thrasher,	1751
George Caswell, Saml. Thrasher, Abel Burt,	1752
Jacob French	1753
Ebenezer French	1760
Samuel Gilbert	1761
Samuel Tubbs, Ebenezer Paul	1763
John Crane, Joseph Burt,	1765
John Hathaway, Shadrach Haskins,	1769
John Paul, Geo. Caswell	1770
John Babbit, Israel French, Abel Crane	1773
James Nichols, Levi French	1777
Ebenezer Mirick, Stephen Webster, Jedadiah Briggs	1778
Simeon Burt	1782
Ebenezer Babbit, Nath. Tobey	1786
Ebenezer Paul,	1790
James Nichols.	1799
Luther Crane, James Dean	1803
George Sanford, John Dillingham, George Shove.	1810
Christopher Paul, Dean Babbit, Apollos Tobey.	1812
Barzillai Crane, Ephraim French,	1816
Barzillai Hathaway, Shadrach Burt,	1817

Levi French, Jabez Fox....................	1823
Adoniram Crane, Saml. French..............	1826
Henry Crane, Tisdale Porter	1829
Milton Paul, Tamerlane Burt................	1832
George Briggs, Alpheus Sanford.............	1835
Nathaniel G. Townsend, Jos. D. Hathaway, ...	1839
Ephraim French, Saml. Newhall.............	1840
Walter D. Nichols, Enoch Boyce,............	1849
Nath. G. Townsend, Nathan Chase, Ebenezer Williams...........................	1852
Thos. Strange, Thos. C. Dean................	1857
Peter Hathaway, ...	1849
William Babbit, Issacher Dickerman..........	1857
Benjamin Crane, Benjamin Luther, John C. Crane	1860
Walter D. Nichols, William Babbit, Simeon Briggs.....................	1862
Thomas C. Dean,..........................	1864
John D. Babbit, Daniel S. Briggs............	1866

TOWN CLERKS.

Abel Burt..........	1735	Asahel Hathaway	1826
Ebenezer Winslow...	1748	Samuel French, jr.......	1827
George Caswell	1751	Adoniram Crane........	1830
Abel Crane.........	1756	Abiel B. Crane..........	1833
John Briggs, jr......	1763	Philip K. Porter	1834
Samuel French......	1765	Ephraim French.........	1835
Ebenezer Phillips....	1767	William S. Crane........	1840
Samuel Tobey	1774	George Crane...........	1849
Stephen Burt.......	1790	Ephraim French....,....	1853
John Crane	1792	Nathaniel G. Townsend......	
Joseph Sanford......	1795	Daniel S. Briggs.........	1863
Apollos Tobey	1798	Daniel C. Burt..........	1864
Adoniram Crane.....	1810	T. Preston Burt.........	1866

REPRESENTATIVES TO THE GENERAL COURT.

None were sent from this town during the first forty years, on account of the expense, as every town was obliged to pay its own representative. Usually, afterwards, one was elected only once in three or four years.

Samuel Tobey, jr 1775, 1776
James Nichols 1779
John Babbit...1788
Samuel Tobey......................1784, 1789, 1792, 1794
Apollos Tobey, 1801, 1803, 1807, 1809, 1811, 1812, 1814, 1819, 1821.
Adoniram Crane 1817, 1818
John Dillingham ....……1824
Samuel French 1825, 1826, 1829, 1830, 1835
Adoniram Crane .. ..……1832
Rev. Thomas Andros.............................1836
Tamerlane Burt.....................................1839
Nathaniel Townsend....................1841, 1842, 1843
Leander Andros ....……1844
Samuel Newhall ....……1845
Abel Baxter Crane................. ....1851, 1864
William S. Crane ....……1859
William Babbit 1861, 1871
Giles L. Leach......................................1852
Samuel Tobey, member of Convention for forming Constitution 1779
Jabez Fox, member of Convention for revising Constitution 1820
Samuel French....... 1853

Senators of the Commonwealth from this town, Hon. Samuel Tobey, Hon. Samuel French, and Hon. Walter D. Nichols.

DOINGS OF THE TOWN.

In 1739, voted that £3 be added to Mr. Tobey's salary. In 1740, not to give John Townsend anything for collecting taxes. Voted to Mr. Tobey £107 salary. For nine months school keeping Mr. Benjamin Paul received from the town nine pounds. 1746, voted to Mr. Toby £150 salary, also voted to build pews in the meeting house this year, to lath and plaster below under the galleries, and mend the glass, and voted £160 for the work; £200 old tenor to the minister, and dismissed the article of building a school house. Committee sent to the General Court to petition that Taunton and not Dighton, shall be the shire town, as some wished. For sweeping the meeting house,

Joseph Babbit received from the town £2 15s. To pay for schooling £6 were voted in 1750.

Mr. Tobey's salary partly paid in farm produce, rye four shillings per bushel; Indian corn, three shillings four pence; beef, two pence per pound; pork, four pence per pound; flax, at nine pence per pound; oak wood, 9s. 4d. per cord. 1751, voted £5 lawful money for support of schools, voted next year £10. John Paul to let the pews in the meeting house and every man to give a note to the treasurer payable in one year. Pews rented on an average for less than one pound.

Voted for schools in 1755, £18; in 1757, £24.

Voted to join in a lottery with Taunton to raise money to clear out Taunton river.

James Macomber and Christopher Paul having been in his Majesty's service, were exempted from taxes.

Voted 1761, to choose four wardens in the town of Berkley in obedience to an act passed by the General Court as a means to prevent the profanation of the Lord's day. Voted to Roland Gavin four pounds, by reason of his having to leave teaching and move out of his house on account of the small pox.

In the eleventh year of King George III, £60 lawful money voted to Mr. Tobey. In 1772 the town is to be divided into four districts and a school house to be built in each, costing $64. May, 22, 1775. Samuel Tobey, Jr., was sent to represent the town in the Provincial Congress, at Cambridge, for six months, the first representative sent by the town to any State or Provincial assembly. He was sent also a representative to the General Court, which met in Watertown, July 19, 1775. £120 voted for schools 1779. In 1793 voted £300 to pay soldiers. and for support of schools; £300, also to enlarge the meeting house by adding fourteen feet.

In 1795 the two fish privileges sold for £38 each.

Various vagabonds or itinerant poor about this time were warned, according to law, to leave town within fourteen days, or they would be proceeded against.

Voted March 5, 1798, to pay the Rev. Thomas Andros in the following articles annually, so long as he shall remain in the work of the Gospel Ministry in said town of Berkley, in lieu of $250, which was the original contract, which was as follows, viz. :

		s.	d.
52	Bushels of Corn at...	3	6
15	Bushels of Rye at	4	0
2	Barrels of Flour at	33	0
12	Pounds of Tea at	2	5
60	Pounds of Sugar at	0	9
18	Gallons of Mollasses at	2	0
15	Cords of Wood at	8	0
5	Tons of English Hay at	4	8
3	Bushels of Salt at	3	0
400	Pounds of Beef at	20	0
500	Pounds of Pork at	4	0
100	Pounds of Flax at	8	0
40	Pounds of Sheep's Wool at	1	6
6	Pairs of Mens' Shoes at	8	0
5	Barrels of Cyder at	6	0
200	Pounds of Cheese at	0	6
400	Pounds of Butter at.	0	8
	Which makes £70	3	
	Also $16 and 17 shillings	4	17
		£75	0

The above articles voted by the town of Berkley at Mr. Andros' own request in writing.

1799. Assonet Neck was annexed to Berkley.

The bell for the second meeting house was purchased by subscription. The weight of it was 635 pounds, and the whole cost was $276. Forty-eight persons subscribed toward its purchase. Samuel Tobey and son paid $41.

Two fish grounds sold in 1803 for $261 each.

In 1806 there were 406 children between the age of four and twenty years in the common schools.

The fund given by Elijah Briggs for the support of the ministry of the first church in Berkley was incorporated in 1813, and when it had increased to $2,000 the interest was to be expended for that purpose. The income of it is now about $150 annually.

Voted, 1819, that a stove may be put in the meeting house. In 1837 voted that the school committee have no compensations for their services.

Aug. 30, 1862. Voted a bounty of $150 for each of the soldiers of the town enlisting for the war of the Rebellion, for nine months' service.

The town officers have managed its finances so well that it is now free from debt.

DATES OF INCORPORATION

of towns in Bristol County in the seventeenth and eighteenth centuries.

Taunton......Sept. 3, 1639.	Dighton.....May 30, 1712.
Rehoboth.....June 4, 1645.	Easton......Dec. 21, 1725.
Dartmouth....June 8, 1664.	Raynham...April 2, 1731.
Swansey.. ...Oct. 30, 1667.	Berkley....April 18, 1735.
Freetown......July, 1683.	Mansfield ...April 26, 1770.
Attleborough...Oct. 19, 1694.	New Bedford Feb. 23, 1787.
Norton........June 12, 1711.	Westport....July 2, 1787.
Somerset..... Feb. 20, 1790.	

In 1800, Berkley contained 115 houses and a population of 1,013, the least of any town in the county. The fifteen towns together contained a population of 33,880.

ROCK HOUSE AND SPRING.

The "Rock House," which was occupied by Robert Sanford, son of Robert and grandson of John Sandford, as his homestead, was an object of interest. It stood on the summit of a rock of broad surface, near the road to Newport. A cavity or hollow in the solid rock, some six feet deep and ten or twelve in width, formed the cellar. The face of the rock sloped away, covering about a quarter of an acre. This house was occupied about seventy years. No one can now tell how or why the cellar was excavated in this manner, or why one should wish to build a house many rods distant from any spring or well. The builder sought evidently to avoid a sandy foundation. There is another house, similar to this, with a cellar cut in the rock, still standing in another part of the town.

Another object of interest, and which has attracted considerable attention, is a spring on the farm formerly owned by Israel Briggs, who, moving to Conway, sold his land to Samuel Philips. This is a mineral spring, which bubbles up an inch or two above the surface. It continues through the year, but is most active in the warm season. The spring, now surrounded by woods, is situated on the east side of the road leading to Pole plain, or rather Poole plain, as it is written in the old records in the Register's office, so called possibly after Mistress Elizabeth Poole, the spinster foundress of Taunton.

MONUMENTUM ASSONETENSE.

The "writing rock," in the lower part of the town, on the farm of David Dean, sometimes called the Dighton Rock, has puzzled the most astute antiquarians. Savans have given four interpretations wholly unlike each other; three of them at least must be incorrect. The lines and figures still remain just what one wishes to call them. General Washington, after examining a copy of the inscription in the museum of Harvard College, expressed his opinion that it was the work of the Indians, having in his early life seen similar writing, which was unquestionably made by the natives.

A French writer, in a learned treatise, read in Paris in 1825, honored it with the classical name given above. Numerous writers have employed folios in describing the rock, but it should be seen in order to have a correct impression of it.

Assonet neck, where the famous rock is situated, was held by the Wampanoags, the tribe over which Philip was king, until 1678, when this territory, conquered from them, was sold by the Plymouth government to the town of Taunton for one hundred and fifty pounds, and subsequently divided among six proprietors. Later the neck was included within the limits of the town of Dighton; but since 1735, that part of it bounded by Taunton River and Assonet Bay was ceded to Berkley.

In 1680, we find the first record of the inscription, given by Rev. Mr. Danforth, who alluded to a tradition existing among the oldest Indians—that there came a wooden house and men of another country swimming on the River Assonet. Within the succeeding one hundred and fifty years there have been taken a dozen or more drawings of the rock. Some of these have been copied in a work, printed at Copenhagen, Denmark, in 1837, entitled, " *Antiquitates Americanæ sive Scriptores Septentrionales Rerum ante Columbianarum in America, etc.*

Some writers state that the inscription is composed of two parts—one cut by the Indians, the other by the Northmen. The latter has been deciphered, and the name of Thorfin, cut in Latin letters, plainly to be read. It is stated that the rock has been purchased by Mr. N. Arnzen, of Fall River, to be presented to the Antiquarian Society at Copenhagen, a weighty gift, eleven feet in length and four and a half in height.

FINIS.

www.ingramcontent.com/pod-product-compliance
Lightning Source LLC
Chambersburg PA
CBHW021026090426
42738CB00007B/920